Original title:
Breeze Between the Islands

Copyright © 2025 Creative Arts Management OÜ
All rights reserved.

Author: Dorian Ashford
ISBN HARDBACK: 978-1-80581-638-6
ISBN PAPERBACK: 978-1-80581-165-7
ISBN EBOOK: 978-1-80581-638-6

Tides of Time and Tangled Roots

Oh, the seaweed dances, so full of glee,
Mimicking jellyfish in a quirky spree.
Coral in tutus sways to the beat,
While crabs on the sand throw a party so neat.

Seagulls are jesters, with beaks full of sass,
Stealing my chips, oh, what a bold class!
Tides pull at laughter like waves on a shore,
As fish gather round for a comedic encore.

Fragments of Whispers in the Air

Fluttering tales from the gulls take flight,
Carrying secrets under the moonlight.
A starfish confesses his love for the tide,
While clams snicker loudly, they just cannot hide.

Whispers of sea foam tickle the crowd,
Spreading old rumors, oh, they're so loud!
With jokes from the depths that leave shells quite sore,
Even the barnacles chuckle, what a rapport!

The Harmony of Distant Echoes

Echoes of laughter roll off the waves,
As dolphins do flips, acting like knaves.
A seal pulls a prank with a splash and a lurch,
While turtles in robes join a wacky research.

The sun throws a party with rays that are bright,
As fish wear their shades, what a silly sight!
Crashing and splashing, the orchestra plays,
With harmonies woven in zany displays.

Threads Between Sunlit Isles

On sun-soaked shores, the tide takes a bow,
While crabs have a meeting, discussing the how.
Sandcastles tumble, like dreams in a rush,
As laughter erupts in a cheerful hush.

Coconuts giggle, rolling down the sand,
While friends chase each other, all hand in hand.
The ocean holds stories that tickle our mind,
In this joyful chaos, pure happiness we find.

Canvas of the Endless Horizon

A seagull stole my sandwich,
I chased it round a palm,
It laughed and flew away,
While I just thought, 'How calm!'

The sky is blue, the clouds are soft,
Yet here I am, quite mad,
Can't help but smile at the chase,
For my lunch, I must be sad.

A crab gave me a wink,
As it danced across the sand,
I tried to join its rhythm,
But tumbled—awkwardly unplanned.

So here's my art, the life I miss,
Laughing in the sun,
Each moment is a funny twist,
Where joy and chaos run.

The Lure of Forgotten Paths

Underneath a twisted tree,
Lies a map drawn by a bird,
It leads to nuts, or so it claims,
But I'm not sure I heard!

I followed lines, all scribbly-like,
Through bushes thick with jests,
I bumped into the local goat,
Who insisted I take quests.

The paths got weirder, that I knew,
With every step I went,
And when I found a hidden pond,
I thought I'd pitch a tent!

But frogs began to croak and sing,
In chorus with the sun,
So here I stay among the fun,
With friends who've just begun.

Journey on the Expanse of Blue

Set sail on a wobbly boat,
Drifting on the waves,
I tried to fish, caught my own hat,
In the sea where chaos braves.

The fishes jumped, all in a row,
Playing tags with me,
One thought my shoes looked tasty,
And swam off with glee.

A dolphin flipped, and gave a wink,
It laughed, or so it seemed,
A sea monster stole my jellyfish,
The boldest of my dreams.

So here I float, a silly sight,
Amidst laughter and blue,
With every splash, I wave goodbye,
To things I thought I knew.

Pathways of Feathered Friends

A parrot squawked at morning light,
'Time for breakfast, mate!'
I held my toast up high and proud,
It tried to steal my fate!

Fluttering wings all 'round my head,
They're plotting, I can tell,
An army of colorful mischief,
In feathery rebel yell.

I set up camp with breadcrumbs out,
Expecting peace to reign,
But finches held a dance-off here,
I lost, time and again!

So I share laughs with my winged pals,
Who chant their silly tunes,
Life is just a feathered joke,
Beneath the sunny moons.

Wanderlust Across Liquid Horizons

A seagull stole my sandwich,
It fluttered off with glee.
I called it a beach bandit,
It honked in mockery.

Palm trees dance in a line,
Like dancers out on cue.
They seem to sway in laughter,
While I search for my shoe.

The sand feels warm and silly,
As flip-flops take a ride.
They vanish to the seaside,
As I chase with a stride.

I build a quirky castle,
With moats of frothy foam.
It leans like my cousin Benny,
When he's drunk and far from home.

Embrace of the Tropical Zephyr

The wind tells jokes of fish,
With whispers slick and sly.
It tickles my sunburnt nose,
As a crab goes scuttling by.

Coconuts are juggling,
They roll from tree to tree.
I swear they're setting up,
A circus just for me.

The hammock sways and chuckles,
As I fumble for a snack.
It's a game of hide and seek,
The chips are on attack.

My ice cream's melting quickly,
It drips upon my knee.
The sun laughs out loud with me,
A melting melody.

Shores of Elysium

I wore my hat like royalty,
It flew off with a grin.
It danced across the water,
Where seagulls took a spin.

The waves play tag with my toes,
And splash me every time.
I swear they're terrible cheaters,
In this watery crime.

A turtle joins the party,
He's moving oh so slow.
I tried to offer him a snack,
But he was "not for show."

The sun makes faces at me,
While I drift on a float.
A paddleboarder wobbles,
Like he's lost his only boat.

Solace in the Colors of Dawn

The sky wears shades of ketchup,
As I rise with a yawn.
I nibble on my toast, now,
While whales sing the dawn's song.

A toucan jokes with parrots,
In vivid colors bright.
They squawk about the sunrise,
While I mix wrong and right.

My coffee tastes like trouble,
I spill it on my shirt.
It joins the salty shoreline,
As seagulls try to flirt.

The morning laughs with mischief,
It twirls around my head.
With every silly moment,
I smile while I'm misled.

Echoes of Distant Shores

Upon the waves, a tale is spun,
Seagulls giggle, having their fun.
Fish in tuxedos dance at dawn,
While starfish clap, their rhythms drawn.

A crab in shades slides by with style,
He winks and shimmies, oh so versatile.
The dolphins laugh, they splash around,
Making mischief, joy unbound.

Currents of Serendipity

A coconut rolls, it has a plan,
To hitch a ride with a jellyfish clan.
They float and twirl, a silly parade,
In sunny waters, sunshine conveyed.

A turtle in sneakers joins the race,
With seaweed hair, oh what a face!
They bump and jostle, giggles galore,
As they tumble and splash to the shore.

Shores Connected by Gentle Winds

The sand whispers jokes as crabs take a rest,
A limbo contest? They're feeling blessed.
With a flip and a flop, they dance with glee,
Who knew crustaceans could be so free?

A pelican sparkles, dreams in its beak,
With stories of islands, he's never meek.
The laughter carries, a treasure untold,
In every wave, friendships unfold.

A Serenade of Flotsam Dreams

Driftwood musicians play a serene tune,
A conch shell whispers, it's time to swoon.
With a plop and a plink, the rhythm begins,
As the tide claps hands, losing its sins.

A pirate fish sings of fortune and fate,
With a hat made of seaweed—oh, isn't it great?
They juggle the shells, those clams in a row,
With a wink here and there, they steal the show.

A Silent Song of Sandy Shores

The sand dunes dance like cheeky kids,
In flip-flops stuck, oh what a bid!
Seagulls squawk in a feathery choir,
While sunscreen turns us into a flyer.

Buckets and spades, our playful gear,
We dig for treasures, laughter we hear.
But crabs steal our snacks, munching with glee,
We shout, "Hey buddy, that's not for thee!"

Wings of the Island Spirits

On wind-swept cliffs, the parrot sings,
Dancing like it's got invisible wings.
With each bright flap, it steals the show,
While we try to keep up, oh what a flow!

Turtles giggle as they plod slow,
While geckos race with a flashy glow.
The sun sets low with a wink and a pout,
Oh island life, what's it all about?

Shifting Shadows of the Endless Pass

The shadows play tag, fleeting and sly,
Leaving giggles beneath the vast sky.
Palm trees wave like they've found a friend,
As we chase sunsets that seem to blend.

A coconut drops, we all scatter fast,
No one wants a bump, that's a blast from the past!
In this game of hide and seek with the light,
We leap and we laugh till we take flight!

Reflections in an Oceanic Canvas

The ocean winks, it's full of tricks,
Mirror ball waves doing slick flips.
Fish play peek-a-boo with bubble hugs,
While crabs put on their best disco shrugs.

We float on noodles, looking so fine,
Sipping on punch that tastes like sunshine.
With every splash, laughter fills the air,
As we try our hardest not to care!

Shadows of Island Dreams

In the shade, the coconuts sway,
Monkeys dance, come out to play.
Tourists trip over their own feet,
While flip-flops make a slapping beat.

Seagulls squawk in a comical tone,
Snatching snacks, they'll claim as their own.
A crab tries to join the parade,
But decides the sand is just too grade.

The sun giggles on golden tide,
As sunburned friends take off to hide.
Laughter echoes from every shore,
As waves roll in and beg for more.

A dog in shades lounges with flair,
While ice cream drips and melts in the air.
In this dance of silliness, pure delight,
Island dreams twinkle under twilight.

Secret Horizons at Dusk

At dusk, the horizon turns peach,
Adventurers gather, it's within reach.
Laughter spills like the waves so loud,
As people pose, feeling quite proud.

The fishermen swap tales, quite absurd,
Of the ones that got away, or so they heard.
A parrot squawks, stealing the show,
With punchlines sharper than a dart throw.

The moon peeks out, just one little eye,
While locals challenge who could fly.
Kites soar high with a comical flair,
As the wind plays tag, pulling at hair.

With each sunset, a joke seems to bloom,
Nature's humor fills up the room.
As stars wink down on the silly scene,
In the magic hour, life feels like a dream.

Murmured Poetry of the Sea

The ocean whispers tales of cheer,
Each wave a joke, for all to hear.
Shells giggle as they roll ashore,
With stories that leave you wanting more.

Fish perform a wiggly dance,
In their scales, reflections prance.
As dolphins flip, they share a grin,
While seaweed tickles, let the fun begin!

A crab with swagger struts about,
With sideways steps, no shadow of doubt.
While boats bounce like beds on the sea,
Add some laughter, and all will agree.

In this watery realm, the fun won't cease,
As waves clap their hands, a raucous peace.
The sea's poetry flows, so rich and free,
With humor swirling like a melody.

Memories Carried by the Currents

Currents giggle, pulling us near,
Bringing back memories, oh so dear.
With floaties bouncing, we splash about,
In laughter and joy, there's never a doubt.

Sandy toes tell tales of the day,
As sunhats tumble and drift away.
Umbrellas dance in the gusts of the gust,
While flip-flops fly, oh, the silliness thrust!

Waves whisper secrets to the shore,
Each tide brings stories, a playful score.
A starfish jokes, 'I'm the real star!',
While sea urchins chuckle from afar.

As sunsets paint the sky bright and gold,
We share our giggles, both young and old.
Riding the currents of laughter and light,
In these waters, everything feels just right.

Embraced by the Horizon's Touch

A seagull stole my sandwich quick,
It flapped away with a daring flick.
I chased it down the sandy shore,
But laughed too hard and fell once more.

The sun was hot, my hat took flight,
It danced around in sheer delight.
With every gust, my sunglasses spun,
I guess this race is all in fun!

The crabs all cheered, I couldn't win,
While fish just giggled, flopping in.
The ocean sang a silly tune,
As I performed my beachside swoon.

In salty air, joy found its place,
With all my toys, just a big embrace.
So let the winds bring laughter near,
Here on the edge, there's naught to fear.

Fleeting Moments in Coastal Light

I built a castle, tall and grand,
But then it melted like ice in hand.
The tide snuck in, oh crafty foe,
And now my tower's quite a low.

A jellyfish did a wobbly dance,
While I just stood in a silly trance.
It jiggled past with such a flair,
I couldn't help but stop and stare.

The sunburnt folks all wore a grin,
As waves of laughter flowed right in.
With beach ball battles, splashes abound,
Our laughter echoed all around.

As the sun dipped low, the sky turned pink,
We laughed about things we didn't think.
In fleeting moments, joy takes flight,
While stars emerged to greet the night.

Between Shadows and Sunlit Waves

The shadows stretched and tickled feet,
As sandcastles framed our goofy beat.
A crab in goggles, oh what a sight,
Danced in the waves with sheer delight.

A kite took off, soared to the sky,
But tangled in a palm, oh my!
With hats that flew and laughter loud,
We chased our dreams behind the crowd.

The sun and shadows played their game,
While flip-flops gave the day its name.
We twirled like dancers on the shore,
With silly poses, who could want more?

In ripples bright, we found our joy,
Just a bunch of friends, oh what a ploy!
With every wave that kissed our toes,
We lived the fun that summers bestows.

The Journey of Wandering Zephyrs

The wind had plans to steal my hat,
It twirled around, oh such a brat!
I ran like crazy, laughter loud,
While seagulls looked on, so proud.

A beach ball bounced from friend to friend,
Our game of catch would never end.
With every throw, a giggle flew,
While sunscreen squirted, what a view!

I saw a fish do a flip and dive,
It looked like it was so alive!
With every wave, the ocean laughed,
As we all joined in its playful craft.

As day turned dusk, we watched the show,
While shadows danced in twilight glow.
With breezy smiles and joy in sight,
We bid goodbye to a day so bright.

The Passage of Ocean Hues

A pelican tried to take flight,
But tripped on a crab and took fright.
With a squawk it did squeal,
What a way to reveal!

A fish flipped and danced with such flair,
Splashing water all through the air.
I chuckled with glee,
At this oceanic spree!

A turtle's slow crawl was a sight,
With a seagull above in mid-flight.
"Race you to that rock!"
Oh what a silly talk!

From waves that do lap with a grin,
To laughter where sea meets the skin.
The ocean's a joke,
In its watery cloak!

Murmurs from Sheltered Havens

A hermit crab wore a new shell,
And danced like it knew very well.
"Join the conch charade!"
In the shade, we all played!

The gulls had a raucous debate,
Over fish that had slipped on a plate.
They cawed and they fussed,
In comical trust!

With seashells, we built quite a fort,
While sandcastles gave us transport.
"Knock it down!" we squealed,
As defenses revealed!

In laughter, the tides swirled around,
With humor and joy they were found.
In shells we confide,
Where silliness bides!

Fleeting Moments in Coastal Light

A crab in a tux gave a wave,
While barnacles sang from the cave.
"Join our jolly dance!"
Gave the fish quite a chance!

A jellyfish wore a crown of green,
And floated while trying to preen.
"Such elegance!"
It's a sight so intense!

Seashells giggled as children did play,
Chasing each wave that would sway.
"Catch me if you can!"
What a fun little plan!

Between whispers of laughter and sun,
The ocean included all in its fun.
With snickers and sighs,
Life's humor complies!

Starlit Reflections on the Sea

Under stars that would twinkle and tease,
A minnow danced low, caught a breeze.
"Look at me!" it proclaimed,
And the night brightly named!

A starfish auditioned with flair,
Changing poses without a care.
"I'm the next big star!"
Oh, how bizarre!

A dolphin leaped high with a cheer,
Each splash, it did shout, "I'm here!"
With flips it amazed,
As we all were dazed!

From twilight to dawn, tales renew,
Where giggles and waves form a crew.
In the dark we find,
Laughter intertwined!

Driftwood Tales of Unseen Paths

On the sandy shore, driftwood grins,
Telling tales of lost sea sins.
A crab named Fred with dreams so grand,
Wants to dance with a starfish band.

The seagulls laugh, they flap and soar,
Sipping saltwater, always wanting more.
As shells make music, oh so bright,
The waves keep whispering, 'What a sight!'

A turtle slow, with rhymes to share,
Says, 'Life's a game, but who plays fair?'
He scores a goal, it's just a mirage,
And slides back out to a hitchhiking barrage.

Windswept Memories of Forgotten Places

In a land where the coconuts giggle,
Old pirates dance and do the wiggle.
A parrot squawks out jokes so old,
While crabs on stilts act mighty bold.

The sunburnt rocks toss around some shade,
While seashells plot a cool parade.
Off they go, despite their shellush ways,
To surf the tides in a grand ballet.

But watch out, friend, there's a fishy twist,
A hungry marlin checks off his list.
He swims right by, in a hurry to snack,
While a lazy octopus takes a time-out back.

Caressed by Ocean's Breath

The waves come rolling, a ticklish tease,
While jellyfish float with utmost ease.
A dolphin leaps, says, 'Life's a splash!',
Chasing fish in a snappy dash.

The sun dips low, a goldfish giggles,
As seaweed sways and brightly wriggles.
The sea cucumbers hold a chat,
About the time they almost got fat!

But here's a twist in our salty tale,
An oyster's secret is ready to unveil.
He's hiding pearls from an old pirate's loot,
While fish cluck loudly, "What a hoot!"

Hearth of the Ocean's Call

In a cozy nook where sand meets sea,
A crab called Carl brews sponge tea.
He invites the gulls for a mid-day chat,
"Who wants to dine on some old sea mat?"

They chuckle and chirp, swapping old tales,
Like the one time a fish wore pails.
The octopus, shy in his funky dress,
Claims he flirts, but it's really a mess.

As the tide rolls in with a sassy sway,
Starfish spin yarns about dismay.
"We lost the beach ball in a tide alarm,
But seaweed hugged it—a lucky charm!"

The Driftwood's Journey

A piece of wood, oh what a ride,
It floats along the ocean's tide.
With fishy friends and seagull calls,
It dreams of land with sandy halls.

It dodges boats with creaky sails,
And dances past the fishy trails.
A hermit crab jumps on for fun,
Together they plot under the sun.

Through whirlpools deep and reefs so wide,
The driftwood sways, a joyful glide.
Each wave, it laughs, it makes a splash,
In every swirl, it's quite the dash.

With every ebb, it tells a tale,
Of foolish fish and windy gales.
So here's to journeys strange and free,
With driftwood dreams on the salty sea.

Lullaby of Fragrant Palms

Under the palms, a soft hum sings,
To lazy lizards and butterfly wings.
Each leaf a pillow, a place to nap,
While crickets play a sweet mishap.

The coconuts roll with a chuckle loud,
As monkeys swing above the crowd.
They steal the fruit, oh what a show,
And tumble down with voices low.

The scent of flowers fills the air,
While all around, there's summer flair.
A lazy sunbeam slips and slides,
Tickling toes of beachside rides.

So close your eyes, let laughter bloom,
In this silly warm, tropical room.
For underneath these swaying trees,
Life's simple joys bring silly glee.

Dreams on Salt-Kissed Waves

A fish with dreams of being a bird,
Flaps its fins and flips absurd.
It squawks and flutters, tries to soar,
While jellyfish giggle from the shore.

The crabs on land throw dance parties,
While watching fish dance blue charters.
But what a sight! They're all a mess,
The ocean's floor, their fancy dress.

They time travel on foam-topped trains,
Riding the laughter through the lanes.
And when they stop, they raise a cheer,
For every wave brings silly cheer.

So if you find a salty crest,
Join the fun; it's simply the best.
In water's arms, we find our way,
Where laughter leads the dance and sway.

Secrets of the Coral Expanse

In the coral gardens, colors play,
Secrets swim beneath the gray.
With clownfish jokes and anemone hugs,
Life's a party; warm like rugs.

The oyster grins with shiny pearls,
While octopuses twirl in swirls.
They trade tall tales of olden days,
Creating legends in silly ways.

Seahorses prance in tiny groups,
Sharing secrets with dizzy loops.
They giggle softly, then take flight,
On currents sweet, just out of sight.

So dive on down, join this parade,
In reefs where fantasy won't fade.
With laughter echoing in every nook,
The ocean holds its secret book.

Constellations on Salted Skin

Under the sun, we spin and twirl,
Catching laughter like a shiny pearl.
Salty kisses and goofy grins,
Counting stars as the day begins.

Seagulls squawk in a playful tune,
Stealing snacks under the lazy moon.
Our toes dig deep in the warming sand,
A fork in the road, should we swim or stand?

Waves crash with an awkward clap,
Splashing us both like a funny slap.
We giggle as we take to flight,
Chasing shadows in the fading light.

Caught in a game of tag with fate,
Running wild until it's late.
The stars above start to align,
Drawing maps that all are mine.

The Listen of Whispering Waters

The water whispers secrets low,
Telling tales we hardly know.
We sip on joy from coconut cups,
Chasing down the mermaids' pups.

Dip your feet and hold your breath,
Avoiding crabs that plot your death.
Giggling wildly, we take a chance,
With fish who think they love to dance.

In the splashes, we find our tune,
Playing drums with the old blue moon.
Each wrong note brings a joyful laugh,
As seaweed tickles on our path.

Riding waves, a playful test,
Skipping seashells like we're blessed.
The ocean sings, our hearts reply,
With every leap under the sky.

Notes from an Endless Horizon

Our feet in sand, we draw a map,
To treasure buried beneath the cap.
Each wave a note, each laugh a chord,
As we compose, together adored.

The sun dips low, a golden tease,
While crabs crawl sideways, doing as they please.
We sing aloud, our voices soar,
With silly tunes that ask for more.

The breeze carries stories far away,
Of pirates lost and games they play.
Side by side, we dream and scheme,
Turning ocean waves into a meme.

Pineapple crowns our heads do wear,
As we prance without a care.
Notes from horizons ever wide,
Laughing as we surf the tide.

The Cool Touch of Distant Whispers

Distant whispers tickle our ears,
As we giggle through our happy tears.
Caught in the game of sea and sand,
We dance like no one else had planned.

Seashells tell of ages past,
While we race to the finish, hoping we last.
Scooping up laughter, we toss it high,
Curly fries in the evening sky.

With every splash comes a new delight,
As friends unite in the fading light.
Fish in the sea, they wink and play,
Encouraging our silliness all day.

The sun says goodbye in a royal way,
As we laugh and shout, "Let's stay, let's stay!"
So here we are, forever found,
In a world where joy knows no bound.

Caress of Distant Shores

A coconut flew past my head,
Chasing seagulls, feeling quite wed.
"Watch out!" I shouted with glee,
As the crab waved back, oh so carefree.

Sandcastles grew like mushrooms—so tall,
Then the tide came in to appall.
We shrieked and laughed, scrambling with style,
As the surf swept our castles a mile.

Fluffy clouds served as fluffy sheep,
While I tried to catch one—made quite a leap!
Fell on my face, but who needs grace?
When laughter fills the glorious space.

The sun wore shades and brewed a cool drink,
I winked at the fish; I think they could think.
As each wave danced with a frothy grin,
Who knew island life could be such a win?

Chasing Soft Currents

I chased a wave that had a trill,
It laughed at me, and oh, what a thrill!
With a splash, it ran, leaving me grinning,
While my floaty unicorn was just beginning.

Every gust of fun tickled my ear,
As I tossed my fears to that frog over there.
He croaked a tune, a hilarious show,
While I tried my best to out-dive the flow.

Salty air whipped through my hair,
Caught a fish; it made quite the glare.
I set it free with a wink and a flip,
It waved goodbye on a slippery trip.

Riding the wind on a tiny sea skiff,
I waved at the clouds, feeling quite swiff.
Laughter chimed in each twinkling spray,
As playful sunshine stole the day.

Echoes of Serene Waters

In tranquil waves, my hat took flight,
As fish giggled, oh what a sight!
The wind wore a smile, skimming the shore,
While I stumbled and tripped, yet wanted more.

Sea turtles danced like quirky old pals,
I joined their groove, now we're night owls.
With jellyfish jigs under the moon's warm glow,
Who knew the ocean put on such a show?

Anchored boats wore silly mustaches,
As mermaids giggled in dive-splashing flashes.
They whispered secrets of sea-sweet cheer,
While barnacles tickled—oh dear, oh dear!

I tossed a seashell to catch a star,
It spun like a top, and then flew too far.
"But it's just a shell!" I called with delight,
As the ocean echoed with laughter that night.

A Dance of Sea and Sky

The ocean twirled its turquoise gown,
While clouds played tag, swirling around.
I danced with crabs in a wild conga line,
Who needs a partner? The sea's divine!

Splashing around, my shoes took a dive,
While a clam laughed, "Oh, look how you thrive!"
The waves wiggled in ticklish fun,
As I clapped my hands—oh, I'm on the run!

With gulls as my backup, we sang a tune,
The sun winked down like a cheeky loon.
All the fish flipped in a broad ballet,
While I spun fast, in carefree display.

The horizon beckoned with a playful tease,
As I chased after where the sky dips and frees.
Who knew such joy in an aquatic ballet,
Could be found in a dance on a sunlit day?

The Call of the Forgotten Isle

A parrot squawks with all its might,
To warn the fish of their first flight.
The crabs moonwalk on sandy banks,
While clams hold parties with food and pranks.

An octopus juggles shells galore,
Dancing with seaweed on the ocean floor.
The seagulls laugh with a knowing grin,
As mermaids sip cocktails made from gin.

A wise old turtle winks and nods,
Simply chilling, avoiding the odds.
The waves carry secrets, but who's to tell?
In this strange place, all is quite well.

So pack your bags, let the journey start,
To the isle of laughter, where joy's an art.
Forget your troubles, leave them behind,
In a land where whimsy is all you'll find.

Lighthouses of Lost Memories

The lighthouse shines with a flickering light,
A beacon for cookies lost in the night.
The candles drift on a funky tide,
As sailors scout for the doughnut ride.

Fish take selfies with silly grins,
While jellyfish glow like electric pins.
With laughter echoing off the tall stone,
It's a party for boats that feel alone.

Wave to the gulls as they do their dance,
While starfish star in their own romance.
Between each laugh a secret lies,
In the splashing fun beneath the skies.

So raise a toast to the tales we spin,
With lights that twinkle where fun begins.
Memories lost are found in the swells,
In a funny world where laughter dwells.

Canvas of Dappled Light

A canvas painted with silly sights,
Turtles wearing hats, what strange delights!
Starfish play checkers on the sandy shore,
Whispering tales, but who keeps score?

Seashells echo with giggles from past,
While colors swirl, an enchantment cast.
The sun sneezes glitter on dreamy waves,
And clams flip pages of comic braves.

Every splash tells a story anew,
As dolphins peak for a vibrant view.
Pirates trade jokes for a treasure map,
Thinking of snacks for their next big clap.

Under the sky, all doubts take flight,
In this painted world, everything's bright.
So gather your humor, join this delight,
In our canvas of joy, dance into the night.

Rhythms of Forgotten Currents

The currents dance with a giggling roar,
While fish tap dance on the ocean floor.
The seaweed waves like it's in a show,
As snails groan loudly, "Oh, take it slow!"

Shells beat drums in a watery jam,
With barnacles joining, a rock-star clam.
Mussels shout "Encore!" between each cheer,
As the waves keep flowing, nothing to fear.

Anemones sway with a funky beat,
While eels hiss jokes that are hard to beat.
In this concert of currents, nobody's shy,
Just keep your fins high and reach for the sky.

From splash to splash, the fun moves along,
In rhythms of laughter, we all belong.
So come and join this underwater scene,
Where humor bubbles, and life's a routine!

Isles of Tranquil Cadence

On a raft of coconuts, I floated by,
Chasing all the clouds that looked like pie.
Turtles turned their heads, gave me a stare,
As if my choice of boat was quite unfair.

Seagulls laughed while trying to be cool,
Diving for fish like they were in school.
I waved to them with a splash from my oar,
They squawked, 'Hey! Not a pool, you silly bore!'

The sun wore shades; it was quite a sight,
As I danced with shadows, oh what delight!
Crabs clapped their claws; they joined in the fun,
Said, 'Dance with us or we'll run, run, run!'

With each ripple, laughter filled the air,
While dolphins played tag in a splashy affair.
As dusk settled in skies of pink and gold,
I felt like a jester, but bold and uncontrolled.

Songs of the Salt Kisses

Salted air tickled my nose and more,
As I tried to catch waves that roared at the shore.
Fish in sandcastles giggled with glee,
While umbrellas danced, sailing sweetly carefree.

A parrot squawked tunes, hip-hop main stage,
Making old crabs break out of their cage.
I tried to join in, but tripped on a shell,
Resulting in laughter that echoed quite well.

Beach balls were bouncing, they joined in the cheer,
As kids built towers with laughter and beer.
Seashells chimed in, oh, one gave a wink,
'Join the fun, don't waste time to think!'

The sun dipped down, turned the skies to fire,
As I spotted a mermaid, my true heart's desire.
She waved and slipped under with a playful tease,
'Thank goodness I'm not made of sand, like these!'

Horizons Brushed by Soft Winds

The sunset giggled, painting skies with flair,
While I pretended to catch the wind's stare.
Kites swooped and dipped, pulled by invisible strings,
I watched my sandwich fly, oh, the trouble it brings!

Fish in the net said, 'Not today, mate!'
As seagulls squawked their own fishing fate.
My sailboat wobbled, too tipsy to steer,
For the wind kept whispering, 'Hey, look, there's beer!'

A crab wearing shades strutted along,
Claiming the beach while humming a song.
'I'm the king of this sand, the ruler with flair!'
I wondered if crabs throw parties, oh where?

The clouds put on hats, as stars took their place,
And jellyfish twirled in a shimmering race.
With laughter in splashes, we painted the night,
In a dance with the waves that felt oh-so-right.

The Language of Fluttering Leaves

A leaf in the breeze tickled my nose,
As I chased it around like a pet little rose.
It winked and it danced, oh, what a sight!
While I swatted at gnats, trying to take flight.

Trees giggled, their branches doing a jig,
As I tripped on a root, feeling quite big.
Lizards chuckled softly, sipping their tea,
Saying, 'Watch your step; that's the oldest decree!'

The sun turned the leaves to gold and to bronze,
While squirrels thumped their chests in a goofy con.
I joined their mad dance and flapped like a bird,
'Nature's a party!' I exclaimed, quite absurd!

With laughter that echoed through canopies green,
As I spun like a leaf, unkempt and unseen.
With a final twirl, I tumbled down low,
For nature whispered, 'You've got the best show!'

The Harmony of Island Solitudes

On shores of sand, a crab did dance,
With silly moves, it took a chance.
A seagull laughed, it joined the fun,
As waves applauded, one by one.

A coconut fell with quite a thud,
The fish swam by, it made a jud.
They chatted loud, without a care,
In this odd show, all thoughts were rare.

The sun peeked in, with a cheeky grin,
It played hide-and-seek, too much to win.
While palm trees swayed, a comic's tale,
Of island quirks, in every gale.

So here we bask, where laughter roams,
Among the waves, we've found our homes.
In island solitudes, joy's our tune,
As night approaches, we'll sing 'til noon.

Pathways Woven by the Wind

A paper boat sailed off to the sea,
The captain, a duck, thought it was free.
With quacking cheer, it set out wide,
While waves had a jest, they'd turn the tide.

The sunbeams giggled, what a delight,
As turtles raced, in silly plight.
They lost their way, still proud, they declared,
Adventure awaits, none was impaired.

A lazy cat tried to join the chase,
But slipped and rolled with a little grace.
The fish just chuckled from beneath the foam,
As laughter spread, we called it home.

These pathways made by a playful air,
Guide us to joy, beyond compare.
With each gust that blows, we're part of the show,
In this grand circus, we're free to flow.

Reflections in a Sunlit Nook

In a cozy spot, the sun did peek,
A squirrel hopped in, feeling chic.
With cocoa beans, it brewed some fun,
While shadows danced, under the sun.

The ocean's waves held secrets tight,
A jellyfish waltzed, oh, what a sight!
Laughs bubbled up from the pearl-gray sky,
As crabs in tuxedos all wandered by.

With sandy feet and hair askew,
The island life felt like a zoo.
The breeze was ticklish, we all could tell,
As seagulls faked a magic spell.

Reflecting joy in this sunny nook,
Where time stood still, and troubles took.
Each giggle echoed, bright as the day,
In this serene place, we danced away.

The Gentle Pull of Restless Waters

Oh, the waters laughed, as they swirled 'round,
Whirlpool giggles, in joy profound.
A fish in a tie recited a joke,
While ducks quacked back, in a muddled poke.

The splashes twirled, like a wild parade,
With seaweed dancing, they would not fade.
Among the tides, a crab threw a fit,
Claiming its throne where it learned to sit.

As the sunsets painted, the sky in gold,
The currents told tales that never grow old.
In our floating chairs, we rested amused,
By the antics of waters, forever enthused.

So here's to the pull, ever so light,
A merry mixture, from morn 'til night.
With giggles and splashes, we wave goodbye,
As moonlit laughter dances on high.

The Silence between Tides

The ocean whispers jokes at night,
Salty air, a tickle, oh what a sight!
Seagulls holding comedy shows,
Dancing on waves, in playful rows.

Crabs wearing hats, they strut and prance,
Tiny pinchers in an awkward dance.
Fish join in, with scales that gleam,
Creating quite a silly scene.

A starfish rolls, it's quite absurd,
As barnacles giggle, without a word.
Shells swap stories, giggling with glee,
In this quiet joke, they all agree.

Moonlight chuckles, lighting the way,
For nighttime mischief, come out to play!
Each ripple a laugh, each tide a sigh,
In the silence, whispers fly high.

Sails of Time on Gentle Waves

A sailboat floats with a crooked grin,
Time ticks slowly, where do we begin?
Windy secrets tickle the sails,
As dolphins gossip with curious tales.

Tick-tock, the waves have a knack,
To dance around like a tidal snack.
The anchor's stuck in a comical game,
Laughing at sailors, who try to tame.

Clouds make faces, puffs of delight,
As sunbeams race to join in the fight.
Swabs of laughter with water so bright,
Every splash a giggle, pure as light.

With each gentle wave, joy takes flight,
On ships of whimsy, we sail into night.
Time's a prankster, it tricks us with fun,
In the ocean's arms, we're never outrun.

Tides of Tranquility

The tides roll in, with whispers so light,
They tickle the sand in a playful bite.
Waves wear shoes made of frothy foam,
Inviting us all to splash and roam.

Seashells shimmer, wearing fine hats,
While playful crabs dance with funny spats.
A seaweed wig with a flair so bold,
Fashioned by currents, a sight to behold!

Floating on laughter, buoyed by delight,
With every smooth wave, the world feels right.
Fishes in disco, under the sea,
Throwing a party, oh come join me!

So let's ride the rhythm, join the parade,
As sunbeams twinkle in an ocean cascade.
Each moment a giggle, a tickle, a tease,
In the tides of calm, we dance with ease.

Colors in Flight

Kites soar high with colors so bright,
Dance in the wind, a whimsical sight.
Each twist and turn, a playful affair,
Laughing and tumbling in sun-soaked air.

Parrots gossip in vibrant schemes,
Painting the sky with whimsical dreams.
They squawk out jokes, full of rhythm and rhyme,
Encouraging laughter, oh such good time!

Sunsets burst forth, in a comedic show,
Orange and pink, where giggles grow!
A canvas of humor, nature's delight,
Colors collide, bringing pure fright.

So let your heart soar, embrace the fun,
In the laughter of colors, we all become one.
With every shy breeze that fidgets and flies,
We paint our joy across ink-blue skies.

Whispers of the Guiding Winds

The seagulls squawk in playful glee,
As kites fly high, wild and free.
A crab in a hat, what a sight,
Dances with joy, oh what a flight!

Palm trees sway, they join the fun,
With coconuts rolling, oh what a run!
A parrot mimics my silly song,
In this island world, we all belong.

The sun sets low, the shadows play,
Laughing fish splish in a random way.
With each small wave, the humor flows,
In this dance, everyone knows!

So grab your pals and hold on tight,
In the playful whirl, we take flight.
As night falls down and stars appear,
We laugh aloud, full of cheer!

Secrets Carried on Salted Air

Whispers of waves, a giggle or two,
As crabs play cards, who knew they grew?
Along the shore where laughs collide,
Even the sand seems to giggle and slide!

A fish in a tux, how dapper and fine,
Invites the dolphins to dance in a line.
The turtles join in with a silly sway,
All secrets shared in a splashy display.

The island blooms with secrets so grand,
As clams share tales with a wink and a hand.
In this madcap world, joy's everywhere,
On the salted air, light hearts declare!

So let's toast to laughter, and craziness here,
With coconuts raised amidst merry cheer.
The sun sets quickly, and the stars align,
In this funny paradise, all's divine!

Lullabies Across the Coral Seas

The waves hum tunes to soothe the night,
As jellyfish glow, it's quite a sight.
Octopus juggling bright seashells near,
Balloons attached, oh dear, oh dear!

A sleepy whale hums a soft lullaby,
As the sea stars twirl with a wink in their eye.
Anemones dance, all in a row,
Keeping the rhythm, putting on a show!

With matters of seaweed, they twist and turn,
While crabs on the sidelines just wait for their turn.
The moon laughs softly, a luminous friend,
In this lullaby land, let the fun never end!

So drift away on waves of sweet sound,
Where silliness in every splash can be found.
With dreams of the ocean and giggles to spare,
Let joy wrap around you, a soft, warm air!

Dance of the Whispering Tides

A hermit crab's shoe, what a wild delight,
Wobbling around like it's taking flight.
Starfish in hats, prancing with glee,
Poking fun at the turtles, oh can't you see!

The tides come in both silly and bold,
With secrets of treasures from legends of old.
They tickle the toes of those who would play,
As laughter erupts, come join the fray!

Twinkle of fish with shimmering scales,
Whispering tales of their outlandish fails.
The sand made of giggles, the foam made of cheer,
In this dance of the tides, joy draws near!

So grab a friend or two, let's all take a dive,
In this wacky world, feeling so alive.
For when happiness calls, we just can't hide,
Together we frolic, where fun's the wild tide!

Floating Dreams of the Forgotten

On a raft made of soda cans,
I sail with my pet, a crab named Stan.
He claps his claws to the rhythm of song,
But can't keep time, so it all feels wrong.

Old flip-flops float like they're on a spree,
Chasing coconut husks on the lemon sea.
Seagulls squawk jokes that make no good sense,
I laugh out loud, share crumbs with the fence.

The sun sets with winks and a wink of a grin,
Even the fish are trying to swim,
They act like they're dancing, oh what a sight!
While jellyfish jiggle with pure delight.

And as night falls, we gather for tales,
Of pirate ghosts and curious snails.
In this floaty world of whimsical cheer,
I found my place, a giggling sphere.

Visions in a Sea of Tranquility

I spotted a dolphin, but it was a shoe,
With eyes made of buttons, it swam right through.
Fins flapping wildly like it owned the sea,
It winked at the sun, shouted, 'Look at me!'

Turtles in tuxedos sip tea on the waves,
Discussing their diets of seaweed and graves.
They argue their taste is the best on the block,
As fish form a band, creating quite the shock.

A crab plays guitar with an artist's flair,
While clams stomp their feet, pretending to care.
Seagulls toss cookies to kids on the shore,
With a wink and a flap, they scream, 'More, more!'

Even the sunsets wear shades made of fun,
As laughter unravels, they race with the sun.
In this tranquil sea, where silliness reigns,
Dreams float on waves, free from life's chains.

Driftwood Tales

A piece of driftwood told me a riddle,
Of how he once played the world's best fiddle.
He claimed he had danced in the moonlight's glow,
While fish cheered him on in a dazzling show.

Sea urchins rolled by with big grins and flair,
Wearing polka-dot hats that they found in the air.
They whispered sweet secrets to sandcastles tall,
Promising good times at the ocean's call.

My flip-flops joined in, hopping 'round in glee,
Trying to salsa with the crabby decree.
But oh! Their rhythm was all out of place,
As I fell in the sand, laughing up at the space.

So gathered we round, sharing snacks of the sea,
With jellyfish jelly and laugh-sweet tea.
The driftwood just chuckled, 'Oh what a show!'
As we danced in our stories, just letting it flow.

A Tapestry of Island Breezes

On mornings so bright, when the sea's full of cheer,
A coconut floated, it giggled, 'I'm here!'
With monkeys in sunglasses, they swung from the trees,
Chasing those waves like they owned the seas.

Pelicans painted in colors so bright,
Crafted a mural that dazzled the night.
They laughed at the stars, 'We're the kings of the show!'
As waves played their music, in sync with the flow.

The sand dunes were pillows for lazy old seals,
Napping in rhythm, dreaming of meals.
Meanwhile, a crab held a banquet so fine,
With shells as his plates and the seaweed a vine.

And when evening came, we'd all gather 'round,
Sharing old tales of the fun we had found.
In this tapestry woven with laughter and dreams,
The islands became punchlines, bursting at the seams.

Starlit Journeys on Water

Stars are winking in the night,
While fish sing songs of pure delight.
A sailor trips, a splash is heard,
He swears he spoke to a flying bird.

The moon does giggle on the tide,
As jellyfish in top hats glide.
With each wave, a tale unfolds,
Of mermaids sharing secret golds.

But wait! A rubber ducky floats,
It quacks a tune 'midst pirate boats.
The compass spins, directions flee,
As laughter dances 'round the sea.

So raise your mugs of salty drink,
Let's toast to all that makes us think.
For every splash and every cheer,
Adventures wait, so let's steer clear.

Echoes of Hope on Serene Waves

Whispers call from the ocean deep,
Where sea turtles snore and fish nap steep.
Seagulls gossip, sharing their glee,
About the crab who lost his key.

A sailor waves as dolphins prance,
While barnacles break into a dance.
Oh, what fun, splash all around,
As snoring shells create a sound.

The anchor's stuck, can't move a bit,
Sailors laugh, it's quite a hit!
They trade their tales of worry and woe,
While hermits giggle, taking the show.

So let's not dwell on sturdy norms,
For folly often dances in storms.
With every tide, let joy resound,
In echoes of laughter that always abound.

The Singularity of Air and Sea

In the maritime, where air gets sassy,
Fish wear hats, and squids get flashy.
The clouds beat drums, they float and sway,
As oysters hum happy tunes all day.

A parrot argues with a flailing kite,
Who insists it's a bird, much to its fright.
But each gust carries jokes from shore,
From old sea ghosts, they never bore.

Surfboards giggle, catching a wave,
While crabs recite the poetry they crave.
Bubbles of laughter emerge with the foam,
This is the sea—our whimsical home!

So let's sail where the antics are grand,
With flips and tumbles across the sand.
For in this realm, both bold and free,
We find the joy of air and sea.

Swaying with the Ocean's Heart

The ocean swirls, a lively dance,
As starfish twirl in a maritime trance.
Crabs wear monocles to see the show,
While seahorses gallop to and fro.

Coconut hats upon our heads,
As waves play tricks on sunburnt treads.
A hermit's shell grows stomach pains,
From eating too many salty grains.

Octopus chefs whip up delight,
With seaweed wraps that taste just right.
While dolphins dive, the kelp does cheer,
Each gust of wind brings giggles near.

So join this fiesta on the briny floor,
Where every laugh brings legends galore.
For in this silliness we find our part,
We sway together with the ocean's heart.

Island Echoes

The parrots squawk in wild delight,
As tourists stumble, their hats take flight.
Crabs dance sideways in their own parade,
While sunburned legs get stuck in the shade.

A fisherman drops his catch with a glee,
While seagulls plot their next big spree.
Sandcastles rise and quickly fall,
As giggles echo through it all.

Jellyfish float like balloons in a race,
While surfers try to keep up the pace.
A dog steals a snack and runs with a bark,
Chasing its tail in a sunlit park.

The sun sets low with a humorous flair,
As beach balls bounce through the salty air.
The waves laugh softly with a splash and a spin,
And everyone knows the fun's about to begin.

Where Waves Rehearse

The tides get ready, they shift and sway,
In surprise, a flip-flop takes off in play.
Seagulls audition for their next big role,
As a clumsy kid trips and loses control.

Shells gather whispers of stories untold,
In a game of tag with the sun, oh so bold.
A beach ball bounces, the kids dive in,
While the sand slips through fingers with a playful grin.

A hermit crab's house needs a stylish update,
In a tiny little shell, it's fashion plate fate.
The ocean sings tunes with a splash and a roar,
While the sun plays peekaboo from the shore.

When dusk draws near, all take a bow,
The laughter lingering under the wow.
Stars twinkle brightly—a raucous crowd,
As waves applaud softly, it feels rather loud.

Symphony of Coastal Whispers

The sea conducts tunes on a sunlit stage,
As children in waves unleash their rage.
Scuttling crabs in their own jolly swing,
While splashy sea-foam claims everything.

Flamingos flaunt, oh what a sight,
Waddling awkwardly, just out of flight.
Sandy toes poke out in the glow,
As people grumble, 'Where did the towel go?'

Kites soar high, twisting on the breeze,
A pop of confetti—oh please, oh please!
Driftwood whispers secrets to the shore,
As waves declare they'd like to explore.

When darkness falls, the lanterns ignite,
And laughter spills out into the night.
Dancing shadows play on the sand,
Where the waves and giggles go hand in hand.

Sentinels of the Shifting Sands

Tall palm trees stand like goofy guards,
As beachgoers juggle their sunscreen cards.
A starfish waves from its sandy throne,
While picnickers munch on snacks of their own.

The sand dunes giggle, shifting with cheer,
As beachcombers find fossils that disappear.
A stray flip-flop grins, as if it knows,
It's got the magic to spark funny shows.

Turtles race with an unhurried style,
While kids envision them running a mile.
The waves clap their hands, a rhythmic beat,
As laughter erupts from every seat.

Under the moon, a curious sight,
Sandcastles glow, twinkling with light.
And all who roam near the shore tonight,
Will find their hearts full of pure delight.

Luminescence of Liquid Pathways

In the water, fish wear hats,
Swimming fast, avoiding chats.
They slip and slide, a slippery show,
Giggling as they dance below.

The waves burst out in silly glee,
Tickling toes of the rowboat spree.
A crab in sunglasses struts about,
While seagulls squawk and twist, no doubt.

The sunbeams shimmer, do a jig,
An octopus plays on a tiny big twig.
Mermaids chuckle, with shells so bright,
As jellyfish glow in the fading light.

All creatures join in this giggling race,
Winking at waves that dance with grace.
A splash, a splatter, oh what a sight!
The ocean's mirrored laughter takes flight.

Whispers of the Tides

A turtle dons a stylish bow,
While dolphins play like they're in a show.
Clams gossip softly, "Did you hear?"
About the mackerel's big fishy fear?

The seashells sing their ancient rhymes,
In the water, they keep good times.
A frog in a hat croaks a tune,
As fish flip their fins, rejoicing soon.

Waves tease the shore with playful shouts,
Splashing sand where the gulls flit about.
A starfish throws a party tonight,
With crabs chasing glowworms in flight.

Tides tickle, tease, and twist, oh why?
The sea spills secrets with a cheeky sigh.
A conch shell chuckles, "What's next for us?"
In this ocean's fun, there's always a fuss!

Currents of Solitude

In solitude swims the quirky fish,
Dreaming of a dinner, oh what a dish!
A stingray dives and suddenly twirls,
While a solitary whale gives a sigh that whirls.

Anemones tickle the lonely crabs,
As they plot silly pranks for the flabs.
A single pelican grins with delight,
Hoping to join in the ocean's invite.

A sea cucumber ponders a dance,
With no rhythm but a brave little prance.
The quiet currents giggle away,
At the fish who forgot how to play.

Yet in this calm, fun lies within,
As solitude brings a whimsical spin.
Secret laughter echoes beneath,
Where each wave knows, joy dwells in sheath.

Gentle Sway of Ocean Secrets

The corals gossip, wrapped in light,
About the shark who lost a fight.
A clownfish chuckles in his bright nest,
While the grumpy pufferfish tries his best.

Sea urchins laugh with spiky finesse,
Playing hide and seek, oh what a mess!
A hermit crab wears a shoe for style,
And walks like a model, if just for a while.

The kelp sways gently, whispers sweet,
Matching rhythms with the seabed's beat.
A dolphin dives, doing flips so grand,
As jellyfish giggle, floating like bands.

Oh, the secrets tucked between the tides,
In every bubble, laughter resides.
With playful antics, the sea does sway,
In the dance of giants, come join the ballet!

Melodies of Solitude and Connection

A seagull's laugh on a distant shore,
Echoes of solitude in the ocean's roar.
Crabs dance in pairs with their pinchers high,
While the fish play tag, just passing by.

A coconut rolls, it's a game of chase,
As tourists slip on sand with a funny grace.
Shells become trumpets for the clams to play,
Merriment lingers in the sun's bright ray.

A wave whacks a fisherman's old straw hat,
He dodges and giggles at a cat-like spat.
Harmony sings from the tides and the foam,
Every splash seems to say, "This is home!"

With laughter as light as the salt in the air,
A smile by the shore—oh, how rare!
Sunsets paint giggles on the canvas of time,
Together we spin, in this rhythm and rhyme.

Pillars of Oceanic Harmony

The jellyfish jiggle, wobbling white,
As the sun plays peekaboo with the night.
Turtles in tutus, twirl with delight,
While otters hold hands, a charming sight.

A sandcastle crumbles, a prince's demise,
As children unleash their most wacky cries.
Waves tickle toes, making everyone squeal,
Ocean's laughter wraps like a warm seal.

Seashells gossip in their rhythmic dance,
Each tiny whisper a comical chance.
Coconuts chuckle at the parrot's quip,
As they roll with glee, on a sandy trip.

Pillars of laughter rise up with the tide,
As fish leap for joy, their secrets they hide.
With each playful splash, they weave a tale,
In this ocean's embrace, let's set sail.

Shores that Sing of Tomorrow

On the horizon, a pirate ship's naught,
Seagulls squawking with all that they brought.
Sandwiches drift from the picnic's bright table,
As lighthearted waves weave a whimsical fable.

Shells narrate stories, glittering and grand,
While the tide takes a bow, as it kisses the sand.
Each grain has a giggle, a tale to regale,
Of mermaids who slipped, and their laughter would sail.

Seashells and surfboards in a bubble parade,
Laughing with crabs as the sun starts to fade.
Egrets on stilts are comedians tall,
In this region where giggles forever enthrall.

Tomorrow awaits with a playful embrace,
As the moonlight sprinkles a silvery grace.
With tomorrows like this, who can complain?
In the dance of the tides, we'll always remain.

Beneath the Canopy of Floating Clouds

Puffy clouds drift like marshmallows above,
Casting shadows on beaches, a treat to love.
Sand from the shoreline sticks to your feet,
As laughter erupts with each comical feat.

Children flinging sand, their giggles combine,
Creating a chorus, in sunshine they shine.
While dolphins choreograph their grand ballet,
Under a sky where funny dreams play.

Kite strings unravel with a tangle in air,
As a sudden gust sends them weaving with flair.
Sunburned noses with joy overflow,
In this joyful habitat, we steal the show.

With the sun as a spotlight, we dance on the shore,
Each wave whispers fun, always wanting more.
Beneath the high skies where we bubble and float,
Every moment a giggle, laughter our boat.

Island Reveries in Gentle Motion

A coconut fell, and what a sight,
Bobbling along in pure delight.
Seagulls laughed at the silly show,
As islanders danced, on toes, aglow.

The hammock sways, a friendly tease,
Inviting naps with the softest breeze.
But sleeping too long leads to odd dreams,
Of fruit that giggles and shakes at the seams.

Crabs in the sand have a waltz routine,
Sidestepping while munching on something green.
Shells clap along, so clackety-heck,
While waves join in with a whoosh and a wreck.

A parrot, dressed up, performs a play,
Dramatizing life in a comical way.
With a squawk and a flap, he steals the scene,
As laughter erupts, filling air so clean.

Threads of Connection in the Night

Stars above twinkle with a grin,
While crickets chirp, their nightly din.
Local cats sing of forgotten dreams,
As lizards join in with their quirky themes.

The moon peeks out, a playful chap,
Shining down on a comically hapless chap.
He trips on a shadow, he rolls, and he falls,
While seaweed giggles from nearby walls.

A dog with a bone finds stealthy delight,
Creeping around in the velvety night.
But the bone's too big, it sends him a-flying,
Through bushes and brambles, he's quite undying.

Fairy lights twinkle along the shore,
Half-lit wishes, who could ask for more?
Connections are woven like strings on a lyre,
As friends share tales by the gentle fire.

The Sound of Stillness on Water

Ripples dance, a silent ballet,
Water so calm, yet full of play.
A fish jumps high, a splashy surprise,
And ducks send waves with their comical cries.

A turtle floats like a floating chair,
Surprised by a splash, he loses his flair.
The frogs croak loudly, a raucous tune,
As if they're rehearsing for a big afternoon.

A leaf drifts down, it takes a curtsy,
Landing on water, oh so flirty.
It bobs and weaves with utmost grace,
While the ripples giggle, in a merry race.

From afar, a distant boat knocks,
Playing tag with the tickling docks.
This liquid world's full of silly dreams,
Where laughter flows like the sun's warm beams.

Oceanic Palettes between Islands

Colors collide in a vibrant scene,
Where the sky blushes a playful sheen.
Mangoes dance with shades of lime,
Creating laughter, dripping with rhyme.

Painted boats flicker like wishes afloat,
Each stroke a giggle, a buoyant note.
The sun drops low and paints the bay,
With swirls of orange, a bright display.

Shells jive together in a sandy band,
Crafting symphonies, ever so grand.
A windswept artist with a wild brush,
Creates a canvas with joy and hush.

As evenings sink in shades of night,
Glittering stars make the scene just right.
Where each vibrant ripple has a story to tell,
Of laughter and colors, where all is well.

www.ingramcontent.com/pod-product-compliance
Lightning Source LLC
Chambersburg PA
CBHW050611100526
44585CB00034B/1408